Original title:
A Symphony of Spruce

Copyright © 2025 Creative Arts Management OÜ
All rights reserved.

Author: Maxwell Donovan
ISBN HARDBACK: 978-1-80567-179-4
ISBN PAPERBACK: 978-1-80567-478-8

Serenade for the Starry Canopy

Underneath the twinkling scopes,
Squirrels gather, bouncing hopes.
They cha-cha on the branches wide,
While owls hoot, their laughter dried.

Pinecones drop like musical notes,
Landing right on fancy coats.
The rabbits dance, a sight to see,
In the moonlight, wild and free.

The Poem of the Pine Winds

In the breeze, a whisper flows,
Telling tales that nobody knows.
A chipmunk prances, quite absurd,
Declaring himself the royal bird.

The trees sway like they're at a ball,
With silly hats, they have a ball.
Ticklish branches scratch the sky,
As clouds float past, and birds all sigh.

Orchestrations of Nature's Breath

The forest plays a quirky tune,
A raccoon strums a silver spoon.
The critters gather, what a sight,
To cheer the moon with pure delight.

Caterpillars tap tap their feet,
While fireflies glow in rhythmic beat.
A rabbit winks, the show's a blast,
With giggles echoing, none are fast.

The Spirit of the Stately Trees

The trees stand tall, a wise old crew,
With leafy caps and vibrant hues.
They tell jokes in the rustling leaves,
While acorns drop, oh how it grieves!

The owls snicker, "Hoo-hoo, what fun!"
As branches wiggle, one by one.
In this merry wood, laughter rings,
With every bark, the humor flings.

Lyrical Leaves

In the forest, leaves were dancing,
Caught in breezes, they were prancing.
One took flight, high with glee,
Landed softly in a tree.

Squirrels watched with eyes so wide,
As acorns rolled, they laughed and cried.
"Not a nut, but leaf ballet!"
Nature's show, come see today!

Chimes of the Cedar Grove

In the grove, the cedars chime,
Twigs strummed sweetly, out of time.
A woodpecker drummed a beat,
Even the rabbits tapped their feet.

A squirrel donned a tiny hat,
Said, "This grooves, can you beat that?"
With every rustle, giggles spread,
While nearby mushrooms bobbed their heads.

The Symphony of Sighs

In the glade, the wind's soft tune,
Made pines whisper, 'We need a boon!'
A frog croaked out a wild refrain,
While crickets chirped in sweet disdain.

The raccoons joined with pots and pans,
Shaking seeds, they made grand plans.
"Who needs silence, we love the noise!"
Their playful chaos brought such joys!

Pines in the Wind

Pines were swaying, laughing loud,
Dancing proudly, they felt so proud.
With every gust, a ticklish tease,
"Who can stand still? Not us, please!"

A hedgehog rolled by in a rush,
Squeezing past with a little hush.
"Keep it down, I'm trying to nap!"
While branches giggled, full of sap!

Beyond the Boughs: An Expedition of Sound

In a forest so tall, where the branches sway,
The squirrels gather round for a wild cabaret.
They strut and they dance on their tiny little feet,
While the birds chirp along to the offbeat beat.

With a nut for a drum and a twig as a flute,
Each critter joins in, what a wacky hoot!
The raccoons chime in with a howling tune,
As the owls twist their heads, saying, "What a festoon!"

A fox with a hat takes the stage with a grin,
Wagging his tail, he pulls everyone in.
The rabbits do flips while the moose plays guitar,
Their music spreads joy near and far.

Through laughter and squeaks, the night echoes bright,
As the stars twinkle down, joining in for the night.
With each silly note, every critter feels free,
In this woodland parade, such sweet jubilee!

Timbered Tranquility

In a wood where the trees do sway,
Squirrels chatter and dart all day.
They'd steal a nut, then trip and fall,
Joking and laughing, having a ball.

A pinecone rolls down the hill,
Dodging the critters with sheer skill.
It performs tricks from branch to branch,
Leaving the forest in a merry dance.

With each gust, the branches creak,
They crack jokes in their leafy peak.
A tree stump giggles, roots all aglow,
Sharing tales of the squirrels' show.

So next time you stroll through the pines,
Look for their laughter, hidden signs.
For nature's giggles fill the air,
In the timbered realm, where joys declare.

The Tune of Tall Trees

Beneath the branches, shadows dance,
Where bunnies hop and squirrels prance.
A tall tree hums a silly tune,
While birds chuckle from afternoon to noon.

With winds that blow and twigs that snap,
They form a band with a leafy cap.
A chipmunk plays a tiny flute,
While ants tap-dance in their fancy suit.

The rhythm sways, a nature's groove,
With every bark, they shake and move.
The elder trees tell jokes so grand,
Keeping laughter in this green band.

So come and join this playful strife,
Where all the creatures celebrate life.
In harmony, they sing with glee,
The tune of nature's jubilee.

Nature's Fading Lament

The leaves start to fall, a slow retreat,
As the trees laugh at summer's defeat.
They shake their branches, a jovial sight,
In golden hues, they bid goodnight.

A squirrel tries to catch one mid-air,
Twisting and turning with clumsy flair.
He crashes down with a startled squeak,
Nature's humor, at its peak.

The winds whisper secrets of seasons past,
Reminding each tree that nothing lasts.
Yet in their sadness, they play a prank,
A leaf drop dance on the riverbank.

So if you hear a tree sigh near,
Just listen close, laughter is clear.
For even in fading, they find delight,
In nature's comedy, all's alright.

Woodland Whispers

In the heart of the woods, whispers abound,
With trees that chuckle, never profound.
Each breeze carries jokes on the air,
While mushrooms giggle without a care.

A raccoon dons a leaf for a hat,
Imitating the woods' crafty chat.
Branches bow low at the bushy parade,
Join the merriment that they've made.

Under the moon, shadows play tricks,
Swaying and dancing with nimble flicks.
The owls hoot in laughter at night,
As critters carouse in the silver light.

So wander the woods with a smile and cheer,
And listen closely, the fun is near.
For woodland whispers are songs of glee,
A secret comedy, wild and free.

Rhythms of Resin and Root

In the forest where giggles bloom,
Squirrels dance like they're in a room.
With acorns bobbing to a beat,
Nature's critters get on their feet.

The branches sway, a funky sway,
While wise old owls look on and say,
"These little moves are quite a treat!"
The woodpecker drums a catchy beat.

Pine cones roll like bowling balls,
Chipmunks dart, down hidden halls.
The sun peeks in with a cheeky grin,
All join the fun, let the games begin!

A fun jam session under the sun,
With every critter getting it done.
So here's to laughter, sprigs on the run,
In our woodsy world, we're never outdone!

The Lush Orchestra at Dusk

As twilight falls, the stage is set,
Beetles buzz, it's a safe bet.
A chorus of frogs joins the fun,
While fireflies twinkle, one by one.

The backdrop hums, no need for lights,
Crickets chirp under starry sights.
With a flute that's made of hollow bark,
Every critter's tuned, ready to embark.

A raccoon plays the tambourine,
His furry hands keep a lively scene.
The raccoon band gets set to launch,
While owls hoot and the shadows prance.

So let's all gather, a wild parade,
Where music plays and worries fade.
Every leaf flutters, a turtledove's plea,
In the nighttime bliss, let spirits be free!

Crescendo of Needle and Sky

The clouds hang low, what a sight,
As pine trees stretch toward the light.
A gust of wind brings a playful sway,
While chipmunks gather for a fun display.

With needles sharp, they strum the air,
Whiskers twitching without a care.
The clouds begin to dance, oh my!
It's a hoedown under the wide, blue sky.

A fox in shades brings the flair,
While bunnies groove, without a care.
The stars come out to join the fun,
An awesome jam that's just begun!

So bring your laughter, raise a cheer,
Nature's show is brilliantly clear.
With every note, our worries drop,
In this hilarious, wild-topped crop!

Treetop Harmonies

Up high amongst the swaying leaves,
Where every branch brings new retrieves.
A parrot's laugh echoes through the air,
While squirrels perform with quite the flair.

A breezy tune, the branches hum,
While prankster winds make the flowers twirl.
Bees buzz along, a sweet brigade,
In this treetop world, we aren't afraid.

The sun dips low, it's Party Time,
Each critter claps to an unseen rhyme.
The glowworms shine, like disco lights,
In our leafy space, oh what delights!

So sway along to the woodland beat,
As laughter echoes, a joyful feat.
With every note, our hearts take flight,
In this funny forest, all feels right!

Whispers of the Evergreen

In the woods, a squirrel chatters loud,
Tiny acorns dropped, a nutty crowd.
Trees in gossip, they bend and sway,
Nature's jabber, here to stay.

Mice hold parties in the fallen leaves,
Chasing their tails, oh, what a tease!
With every gust, they dance and twirl,
Even the trees give a little whirl.

Melodies in the Canopy

A woodpecker knocks on a tree so tall,
Bouncing beats like a funky ball.
Branches sway, like a band on stage,
Rustling leaves turn the forest page.

A rabbit hops, in rhythm, so spry,
Ears flopping like they're ready to fly.
Trees hum tunes on a breezy night,
The stars above say, 'What a sight!'

Harmonies of Pine and Mist

In the mist, the creatures sing,
Jays are jiving, oh, what bling!
Feeling fancy, a deer does prance,
Nature's stage, the wildest dance.

Breezes tickle the pine's tall hair,
Every whisper says, 'Dance, if you dare!'
Mossy rocks groove, they join the fun,
By the moonlight, the frolicking's won.

The Forest's Lullaby

A sleepy owl gives a hoot and yawn,
Critters snuggle up on the lawn.
Crickets chirp a quirky tune,
As the night slips by, beneath the moon.

Twinkling lights from the fireflies bright,
They flick and flitter, what a sight!
The trees sway gently, as if they knew,
All their secrets shared, just me and you.

Melodies of Verdant Pines

In the forest, trees do sway,
Singing tunes both weird and gay.
Squirrels dance with acorn hats,
While birds take turns at silly chats.

The breeze joins in with a hee-hee,
As branches twist with glee, you see.
A woodpecker drums a funny beat,
While raccoons shuffle on little feet.

Each fern late-night throws a party,
Inviting creatures, oh so hearty.
They frolic 'neath the twinkling stars,
In a world where laughter's never far.

The moon peeks in with a chuckle low,
As critters hit the dance floor flow.
With wind as DJ, spinning tunes,
In the forest, where joy festoons!

Echoes Among the Evergreen

Whispers through the evergreens,
Paint a picture of all things funny.
A fox puts on a hat so bright,
Claiming he's a wizard tonight.

The trees decide to throw a ball,
Inviting critters, one and all.
Mice wear shoes made out of leaves,
With secret moves that no one believes.

A badger croons a goofy song,
Says, 'Come dance, you can't go wrong!'
Each branch sways in a merry way,
Encouraging frolics 'til the day.

With echoes bursting in the night,
The woods erupt in pure delight.
A party groove beneath the sky,
Making laughter zip and fly!

The Dance of Pine Needles

Pine needles twirl in wild delight,
Wobbling under the soft moonlight.
A chipmunk leads with fancy flair,
Dodging shadows everywhere!

A nuthatch scats some jazzy notes,
While old logs serve as lively boats.
They glide upon a gummy swamp,
With frogs providing a funny stomp.

Tree trunks tap along in time,
While squirrels keep the beat in rhyme.
Each rustle brings another laugh,
As branches wave like a friendly gaffe.

The dance goes on, it never ends,
Nature and joy are the best of friends.
In every step, a whimsy's found,
In the cone-strewn stage of the woodland ground!

Harmonies of the Forest Floor

Mushrooms giggle, play hide and seek,
While wormy wigglers dance to the beat.
Beneath the trees where shadows creep,
A chorus of critters, awake from sleep.

The sounds of laughter echo clear,
As beetles juggle a couple of pears.
They tumble and roll in a grassy patch,
Making funny faces with each little catch.

Every pine cone has a tale to share,
Of adventures they had, beyond compare.
Singing 'bout all their windy flights,
And mischief they caused on starry nights.

So listen close to the forest hum,
It's filled with joy and enormous fun.
As nature orchestrates a merry song,
In this lively world, you can't go wrong!

Echoes Beneath the Boughs

In the woods where squirrels play,
The conifers dance in a sway.
They wiggle and jiggle with glee,
Singing songs as wild as can be.

A chipmunk jumps, a fox joins in,
They form a band with a cheeky grin.
The branches sway, the leaves all cheer,
While raccoons tune a tune that's clear.

A deer prances, stealing the show,
With a graceful step that's a bit too slow.
But laughter rings from tree to tree,
As nature hums its melody.

So if you wander where critters play,
Join the chorus, don't delay.
Under the boughs, find your joy,
In a laugh-filled woodland ploy.

Coniferous Cadence

The pines wear hats made of snow,
While the windy giggles start to blow.
A woodpecker drums without a care,
As rabbits twirl in the frosty air.

With every swish of a leafy crown,
The forest floor becomes a clown.
Mice breakdance, and owls hoot loud,
As stitches upon laughs weave a shroud.

The frogs join in with a ribbit tune,
Underneath the lazy afternoon.
A fox becomes a sultry star,
While squirrels cheer, 'You've come so far!'

Even the logs are rolling near,
As thumping beats conquer all fear.
In the woods, where fun takes flight,
Each bark sings out in sheer delight.

The Song of Tall Pines

Beneath those towering green heights,
The tallest trees hold funny sights.
With acorns flying like confetti,
It's a party where none are petty.

Owls wear glasses, quite a sight,
While beavers dance in pure delight.
Raccoons prance, tails high in the air,
With antics that are beyond compare.

The sun peeks through in playful beams,
While critters bounce like in wild dreams.
A bear taps its toes to the beat,
As nature's party gets on its feet.

When shadows stretch and laughter rings,
You'll find joy in the forest springs.
Each gust of wind, a playful tease,
Bringing smiles to all with ease.

Serenade of the Silent Woods

In stillness reigns a giggling breeze,
Whispers tumble among the trees.
Each twig snaps with a cheeky dance,
While critters prance in a merry trance.

A hedgehog sings with a prickly charm,
Enticing all with its quirky drama.
The squirrels quiz, 'Have you heard the news?'
With bated breath, they share their views.

Hooting owls join a late-night show,
While raccoons steal snacks on the go.
Each leaf flutters with laughter's delight,
As creatures jive under moonlight.

From branches high to the forest floor,
Echoes of chuckles, we can't ignore.
In the silent woods, a raucous tune,
Springs forth like blooms in the light of the moon.

An Overture of Green

In the forest, trees they dance,
With a sway and jig, they take their chance.
Squirrels play the drums, you see,
While birds harmonize with glee.

Butterflies twirl in the autumn air,
Mixing colors everywhere.
The breeze joins in, it sounds so fine,
A wacky tune from pine to pine.

Acorns fall like clumsy balls,
As laughter echoes through the halls.
A raccoon sings in offbeat tone,
While the pinecone family plays alone.

The sun shines bright, it winks in fun,
Nature's stage, a show begun.
With every rustle, there's a cheer,
In this green world, joy is near!

The Euphony of Trees

Branches stretch with silly glee,
Every leaf a part of the spree.
The wind whistles a quirky tune,
While owls hoot at the afternoon.

Mice conduct their tiny band,
Playing notes with little hands.
The pine trees sway, like they're free,
Bouncing to the rhythm, oh so carefree!

A wooden flute made from a twig,
Creates sounds that are pleasantly big.
Raccoons tap-dance on the ground,
As laughter and music twine around.

In this orchestra where nuts abound,
Nature's joy is clearly found.
Messy melodies fill the air,
An endless concert everywhere!

Nature's Trilling Heartbeat

The crickets chirp a silly hum,
While dandelions dance, oh-so-glum.
Beetles march with a heavy beat,
Their comedy acts are quite a treat.

The brook bubbles with playful jests,
As frogs croak in their fancy vests.
The sunbeams laugh, they bounce around,
In this lively world, joy's always found.

Every gust a chuckle shared,
With trees listening, never scared.
In this green expanse, jokes unfold,
Nature's fun is a sight to behold!

As seasons shift, the laughter stays,
In rhythm with the sun's bright rays.
With every rustle, a jolly cheer,
A heartbeat of joy, loud and clear!

The Pulse of Spruce and Sky

Under the azure vault up high,
Frogs are singing, oh my, oh my!
Clouds drift by, in fluffy parade,
While trees break into a silly charade.

The pine needles rustle, giggle and tease,
Making music with every breeze.
Chirping birds join the fun,
While shadows dance in the bright sun.

Nature's fairies, all wearing green,
Waltz through the branches, a whimsical scene.
As branches jive and roots take a bow,
The joyous ruckus is happening now!

So gather 'round, let spirits lift,
In this world, we share the gift.
With laughter and joy, the sky swings low,
In the heart of green, we steal the show!

Chants of the Woodland Spirits

In the forest, squirrels prance,
Chasing shadows, what a chance.
Acorns flying all around,
Nature's dance, the funniest sound.

A rabbit hopping, trying to sing,
Off-key notes make the spirits spring.
Mushrooms giggle, towering tall,
Who knew woods could be this small?

A chipmunk strums on a tiny lute,
While owls hoot in a sharp suit.
Fairies chuckle, losing their way,
In a whirlwind of leaves, they sway.

The trees sway low, whispering jokes,
A fox laughs loud, joining the folks.
Winds carry giggles through the night,
Woodland spirits, pure delight!

Ballad of the Timberland

In the timberland, trees do cheer,
With every breeze, they crack a leer.
Pinecones roll, adding to the fun,
While raccoons plot, oh what a run!

Woodpeckers drum, making a beat,
Squirrels dance, tapping their feet.
A bear grins wide, sporting a hat,
All join in, where's the mat?

The brook giggles, splashing along,
Even the rocks hum a silly song.
A moose tells tales, big and grand,
While trees do clap, so close at hand.

Even the shadows, they twist and play,
Making shapes that dance and sway.
In the timberland, laughter's the king,
Join the fun, let your heart swing!

Resonance of the Roots

Roots below, tangled in chat,
Gossiping 'bout the things they've sat.
Worms tell stories, wild and bold,
About the secrets they behold.

The breeze tickles, making trees giggle,
As tiny ants begin to wiggle.
"Who's the tallest?" one vine asks,
While blades of grass don their masks.

Through the soil, a pun is heard,
Twirling up like a cheeky bird.
Fungi snicker, bursting with cheer,
With every joke, their caps appear.

Roots reach deep but laugh so loud,
As branches sway, they feel so proud.
In this place where tickles flow,
A funny world, where all can grow!

Hymn to the Hidden Grove

In a hidden grove where mischief brews,
The flowers wear the silliest shoes.
Trees lean in to share a jest,
While butterflies join in the fest.

A raccoon's mask, so sly and neat,
Plays the role of the clever cheat.
With twinkling eyes, it steals the show,
Stealing snacks in a comical flow.

The crickets chirp a laugh track now,
As frogs croak out a jovial wow.
The moon peeks in, winks in delight,
As stars join in this cheerful night.

Laughter echoes through leafy trees,
With every tickle from the breeze.
In the grove, where joy is rife,
Nature sings, full of life!

Nature's Orchestrated Embrace

In the forest where we play,
The trees must dance each day.
With branches swaying side to side,
They're the band we can't abide.

Squirrels leap from bark to bark,
Playing music in the park.
The leaves join in with a rustle,
Chasing crows, oh what a tussle!

Raccoons tap a funky beat,
While the owls flap their winged feet.
Even deer join in the fun,
Waltzing 'neath the golden sun.

So let's rock beneath the trees,
With the breeze and giggling bees.
Nature laughs and hums a tune,
Join the chorus, morning's boon!

Chords of the Evergreen Woods

In the woods, the echoes ring,
Listen close, the trees can sing.
A pinecone launching, oh what flair,
Splat on head, without a care!

Birds are chirping, "Do-re-mi,"
A woodpecker's got the beat, you see.
But whispered notes, the squirrels tease,
Off-key humor in the breeze.

Below the boughs, the critters play,
In their band, it's really gay.
They strum on roots, beat on stone,
Nature's laughter, fully grown.

With every rustle, shake, and twirl,
The tallest firs begin to whirl.
Join this dance, don't be a fool,
The forest's groovin', what a school!

Rustling Aspirations

Pines are stretching, trying hard,
To reach the sky, they dance, they guard.
A gust comes in and shakes their crown,
Leaves them dizzy, twirls them down.

Beetles tap on tree trunks tight,
To find the groove, they work all night.
With every crack, they jammed so bold,
Their tiny parties never get old.

The shadows wiggle, branches sway,
In this glade, the critters play.
Chipmunks twirl, with acorn hats,
Dancing jigs with furry rats.

So if you hear that rustling sound,
The woods are laughing all around.
Join the fun, feel life's embrace,
In the forest's wild, zany space!

The Pine's Whispered Tune

The pines are swaying, what a sight,
Whispers float in dappled light.
Branches bending, having fun,
A secret dance, just begun.

The breeze brings jokes from tree to tree,
"Why did the sapling flee?"
It heard the lumberjack's loud laugh,
And thought it wise to take a path!

Nearby, a lizard joins the show,
With a tap of toes, a little glow.
While ants conduct with tiny flair,
Creating tunes beyond compare.

So listen closely, if you can,
Nature's humor, oh so grand.
The pines' sweet whispers, joy in bloom,
In laughter's arms, there's always room!

Serene Interludes

In the woods where squirrels dance,
A rabbit slips, just missed his chance.
Caught off guard by a gusty breeze,
He tumbles down with perfect ease.

A bear sings low, a tune so bold,
While hedgehogs snicker, tales retold.
The owls hoot, a chuckling sound,
As nature's clowns spin 'round and 'round.

The Sound of Solace

Pines whisper secrets, sharp and clear,
While frogs croak loud — now isn't that queer?
A chipmunk's giggle, a soft little tease,
As he scurries by with the greatest of ease.

A moose tries to dance, but trips on a log,
The trees all shake — they start to hog.
Nature's laughter rings through the glen,
As critters plot their next big zen!

Woodland Rhapsodies

A porcupine plays in prickled delight,
While fawns chase shadows, oh what a sight!
The wind plays guitar with a rustling tune,
While raccoons party beneath the bright moon.

The chatter of creatures fills up the night,
A beaver brings snacks — oh what a delight!
With every chuckle, the forest does sway,
In this merry jest, old troubles decay.

Melodic Murmurs Amongst the Pines

The cuckoo calls out, 'What time is it now?'
While all of the rabbits just take a bow.
A lizard struts, proud of his show,
As ants march by, in elegant row.

Squirrels strike chords with acorn-capped hats,
While the hedgehogs tap dance among scattered mats.
With giggles and wiggles, the forest does cheer,
In this woodsy wonder, there's nothing to fear.

Trills in the Tall Trees

In the forest, a bird takes flight,
Flapping wings, oh what a sight.
Squirrel tries to dance with flair,
But trips on roots hidden there.

Branches sway to a jolly tune,
Bouncing leaves beneath the moon.
The wind chimes in with a laugh,
As trees shake hands with a photograph.

Frogs croak loudly, a froggy choir,
Barking bark beetles stoke the fire.
With each note, the critters spin,
Creating a symphony from within.

Among the trunks, a party swells,
Fungi whisper their secret spells.
So when you walk, feel the breeze,
Join the concert amongst the trees.

The Choir of Conifers

Pine needles hum a soft refrain,
While old oaks tease with jokes again.
In the choir, they're raising cheer,
Whispering secrets for all to hear.

Under clouds, the trees all sway,
Chattering gossip throughout the day.
A lonely crow tries to sing high,
But his notes just make the squirrels sigh.

The roots keep tapping to the beat,
As the chipmunks scurry on tiny feet.
Everyone seems to take a seat,
For the performance of nature's elite.

A woodland show, both strange and bright,
With hiccuping frogs in the spotlight.
Each critter bold, and quite absurd,
Sings along, a merry herd.

Notes from Nature's Heart

Beneath the sky, oh what delight,
The trees sport hats, quite a sight.
One wears pine, another a sprout,
While critters laugh as they dance about.

Acorns fall with a plunky sound,
Making music upon the ground.
A raccoon plays the tambourine,
While the bushes shake in between.

A dandelion sways, so brave,
Pretending to be a rock star wave.
Flowers join with a floral twist,
Creating beats that can't be missed.

Deep in the woods, let laughter flow,
For nature's jokes are quite the show.
When leaf and twig strike up a chat,
You'll find the funniest tales, imagine that!

Crescendos in the Green Realm

In a glade, the instruments mix,
With twigs and leaves, the forest picks.
A deer comes in with a gentle leap,
Joining the fun while others sneak peep.

The laughing brook tunes up its flow,
While beavers beat a rhythmic show.
Hummingbirds zip in a bright blur,
Adding a spark with each little purr.

Rabbits drum with their twitchy ears,
Creating echoes, converting cheers.
Sound waves ripple through mossy grooves,
As the forest joins in, each heart moves.

Let's dance, dear friends, where the wild grows,
To melodies only the woodland knows.
When the sun sets, the laughter glows,
In this lush arena, joy only shows.

Overture of the Autumn Boughs

The trees are dancing, how absurd,
With limbs that sway to tunes unheard.
Leaves laugh as they fall, what a sight,
They twirl and spin in pure delight.

Squirrels audition with acrobatic flair,
Chasing each other without a care.
A nutty ballet on a high branch,
Wiggling and jiggling, ready to prance.

Mice in tuxedos, they join in too,
Waltzing with pinecones in their shoe.
Nature's own folly, their stage so grand,
A woodland gala in the soft, cool sand.

The sky joins in, with clouds as the band,
Raindrops tap dancing on leaves that stand.
Autumn's rehearsal, a funny charade,
In the forest's embrace, a wild parade.

Sounds of the Saplings

Tiny sprouts whisper secrets low,
In a language only the ferns seem to know.
With giggles of grass and chuckles of thyme,
They plot their mischief, oh, what a crime!

Saplings trade stories, what a delight,
Of sun-soaked mornings and starry night flight.
They wiggle their roots to the rhythm they feel,
Creating a concert, all vibrant and real.

The wind is their audience, rustling with glee,
It lifts them a bit, oh, wild and carefree.
Each branch is a trumpet, each leaf a sweet drum,
To the symphony of laughter, the saplings hum.

Caterpillars join with their smooth slinky moves,
Crickets provide beats in the grass as it grooves.
Together, they frolic in bright midday light,
In the laughter of nature, a pure, silly sight.

The Gathering of Pine Spirits

Pine spirits gather, each with a grin,
Swapping tall tales of where they've been.
From mountain tops high to valleys so fine,
Their laughter resounds like a merry wind chime.

"Remember that time," one proudly did boast,
"Of a squirrel who tried to hop on a toast?"
The others erupted in fits of pure glee,
Imagining squirrels with jam and green tea.

A breeze blows in, tickling their needles,
Challenging them to bounce like the beetles.
With every rustle, they dance and they sway,
As shadows jiggle, they join in the play.

From dusk till the stars brightly start to twinkle,
They chatter and chuckle, a delightful crinkle.
At midnight, they twirl, oh what a spree,
These pine spirits revel, wild and so free.

Nature's Melodic Embrace

In the meadow where giggles collide,
The flowers hum softly, never to hide.
They sway together, a colorful choir,
Singing the songs of the world's deep desire.

Butterflies flutter in sequined attire,
With moves so bold, they ignite the fire.
A ladybug leads, with spots well aligned,
As petals applaud, all completely entwined.

Bees join the rhythm with hearts full of cheer,
Dancing on daisies, no worry or fear.
Sweet nectar delight, a feast in the air,
A buffet of joy, their worries laid bare.

With turtles tapping their little shells tight,
The forest rejoices in pure, silly light.
Nature embraces this playful display,
In a world full of laughter, come join the ballet!

A Waltz Among the Pines

In a grove where trees do sway,
Squirrels dance and leap all day.
Mice on toes, they twirl around,
To a silly tune, they all are bound.

Branches sway to a bouncy beat,
A hedgehog joins, short on feet.
Frogs in tuxedos croak their song,
While a raccoon hums all night long.

Leaves are clapping, what a sight!
Fireflies twinkle, oh so bright.
Bunnies hopping, rhythm divine,
Under the stars, a joyful line.

As the music starts to fade,
Dancing critters, unafraid.
With a bow and little grin,
They take a bow, let fun begin!

The Choir of the Forest

In the forest, noises cheer,
A choir sings from far and near.
Birds with notes a bit off-key,
Chirp along, it's harmony!

Bears try to dance, but trip and fall,
Making everyone laugh, that's all.
Trees sway gently, keeping time,
While ants march in a single line.

A wise old owl, he tries to lead,
With a wink and a funny deed.
The stars above begin to shine,
As raccoons play tambourine, so fine.

There's no maestro, just pure fun,
Nature grinning, everyone.
In this choir, all are bold,
With laughter sung, let's be consoled!

Resonance of the Wild

In the wild, a sound does roam,
Bees buzzing loud, they call it home.
A playful fox with wiggly tail,
Jumps and prances, without fail.

Horns of elk, they toot and honk,
While lazy bears just sit and conk.
Chirping crickets join the noise,
A happy ball of woodland joys.

Overhead, the hawks will squawk,
Raccoons giggle and have a talk.
Every rustle, every squeal,
Adds to laughter, oh, what a thrill!

As night falls, the echoes play,
Funny tales of a wild day.
With every sound, a secret shared,
In this place, no one despaired!

Lullabies in Woodland Shadows

In the shadows of the trees,
Silly stories float on the breeze.
Crickets sing a funny tune,
While owls hoot at the bright full moon.

Frogs are crooning by the lake,
Each voice unique, a silly quake.
Tumbleweeds roll, giggling along,
To the whisper of the night's sweet song.

Bunnies snuggle in the grass,
Dreaming of the acorns they amass.
A raccoon sneaks, with eyes aglow,
Stealing snacks from the woods below.

As dreams drift through the dappled night,
Nature hums with pure delight.
In every nook, a chuckle hides,
In woodland shadows, laughter abides!

The Ballet of Branches

Branches sway like dancers,
In the wind's playful prance.
Twigs twist and bend with laughter,
In a nature's silly dance.

Leaves clap their tiny hands,
Cheering for the trunk's bold spin.
A squirrel joins, taking a chance,
In this leafy, uproarious din.

The sunbeams spotlit the stage,
While shadows twirl and whirl.
A pine cone rolls off in rage,
For not being part of the swirl.

Nature's show, a feathery fling,
With pine needles as confetti.
Oh, what joy this dance can bring,
In the forest, bright and merry!

Rustic Rhapsody

In the woods, a tune is made,
With a kooky, chirpy beat.
Branches thrum like a charade,
While acorns bounce on tiny feet.

The chipmunks play their saxophones,
Pine boughs form a rhythm line.
Even the moss hums to the tones,
With laughter that's just divine.

Fungi dance like disco queens,
Underneath a dappled light.
Roots join in with silly routines,
Leaving squirrels giggling outright.

Nature's joke has no refrain,
Just playful notes that intertwine.
In this raucous, rustic lane,
Life's a comedy by design!

Enchanted Green

In the glade, the mossy floor,
Tickles toes with every step.
The ferns whisper tales galore,
    As creatures plot and inept.

Will-o'-the-wisps giggle bright,
Guiding folks on a wild quest.
A hedgehog dons a hat tonight,
    Saying, "I'm the very best!"

Vines twist in a comical way,
Like they're trying a new dance.
Every bough has come to play,
    In this lively forest trance.

Laughter echoes through the trees,
As nature joins the jolly spree.
Every rustle brings a tease,
    In this enchanted jubilee!

Vibrations of Verdant Vistas

The forest hums with giggles light,
In a chorus vast and free.
Breezes carry jokes in flight,
With pine scents as the glee.

Trees shake hands, they twist and twirl,
As if they're having a ball.
Moss carpets soft for every girl,
Who joins in on this carefree call.

A bunny hops with tunes to share,
While earthworms groove below.
With laughter floating in the air,
Even the flowers start to glow.

Nature's melody, sprightly cheer,
Brings forth a smile from me to you.
In this green haven, joy draws near,
With every high note ringing true!

The Gentle Chorus of the Wilderness

In a forest where trees play chess,
Squirrels plot, don't you guess?
With acorns as their prized pawns,
They dance at dusk, beneath the dawns.

Birds sing in off-tune delight,
As raccoons join the chirpy fight.
Mice recite their little prose,
While badgers stomp in funny clothes.

A moose with shades struts down the lane,
Fashion goals, oh what a gain!
He winks at owls with glasses thick,
Their wisdom wrapped in awkward tricks.

So join this jolly woodland show,
Where laughter rises, sweet and slow.
The trees may sway, the critters prance,
In this wild waltz, all take a chance.

Evergreen Elegy

The spruces whisper tales so grand,
Of mushrooms wearing hats, not planned.
A chipmunk juggles nuts with flair,
While a porcupine takes a chair.

Each twig a baton in sprightly hands,
Conducting chaos across the lands.
Bees buzz with a comic tune,
As awkward frogs croak under the moon.

A pinecone drops, a sudden scare,
Turns out, it's just a baby bear!
With fur so fluffy, eyes so wide,
He joins the band, now it's a ride.

So let's laugh with ferns and moss,
In this green gig, we're never cross.
For nature's stage is full of cheer,
Where even the tallest trees can leer.

Echoing Through the Pines

Amidst the pines, a ruckus grows,
Gophers wear the latest clothes.
With dandelions as their crowns,
They twirl around, like little clowns.

A beaver's dam, a grand display,
Of leafy green and bark ballet.
The fish jump high to catch the show,
While turtles cheer, 'You go, you go!'

Each echo in this leafy dome,
Squeaky laughter finds a home.
Raccoons in tuxedos strut,
While owls hoot, 'What a nut!'

So join this woodland, don't delay,
Where humor blooms in nature's sway.
Underneath the emerald hue,
The funny side of life rings true.

Resounding in the Green Heart

In the heart of the forest, giggles collide,
As squirrels and rabbits take a wild ride.
With acorns bouncing like popcorn popped,
A comedy show, never stopped.

A drumming bear with a rhythm divine,
While raccoons dance in a conga line.
They twirl and swirl 'round the big old oak,
Cackling loudly at each silly joke.

The shadows play tricks, the branches bend,
As deer tell tales that never end.
Frisky foxes slip and slide,
Amidst the laughter, joy's the guide.

So in this green heart, let's all unite,
To celebrate nature's sheer delight.
For every giggle and playful stunt,
Is a reminder that life's a fun front!

Serenade Under the Stars

In the forest where the critters dance,
A squirrel sings with a nutty romance.
The owls hoot in musical delight,
A raccoon joins in, a bandit at night.

The fireflies flicker, a note of cheer,
While the frogs try to croon, oh so severe.
The crickets conduct with a faint, raspy tune,
As the moon beams down like a joyful buffoon.

The badgers tap their feet to the beat,
While the hedgehogs roll in a jazzy retreat.
With a wink and a nod, the forest goes wild,
A concert so quirky, it's nature's own child.

So come join the fun where the laughter sways,
In this merry hush, where all creatures play.
Under twinkling stars, the night never ends,
In a musical world where the whimsy transcends.

The Crescendo of Wind through Branches

Whispers of breeze play a cheeky tune,
Rattling branches, making trees swoon.
The leaves chuckle, rustling in glee,
As the wind breezes whispers, "Come dance with me!"

A chipmunk leaps, thinking he's grand,
As he twirls and tumbles on this windy band.
Even the pine cones, swinging in might,
Join in the fun, taking flight in delight.

Sounds of the forest, a symphony light,
The squirrels play tag, chasing shadows at night.
With giggles all around, what a sight to behold,
As the sweet serenade of branches unfolds.

Each gust brings laughter, a twist of fate,
While the old trees chuckle, "Ain't life just great?"
Nature's rhapsody filled with silly cheer,
In each whirling dance, we find joy, oh dear!

Rhythms of the Woodland

A woodpecker drums on a hollowed-out tree,
While the rabbits join in, as sprightly as can be.
The deer prance to the beat, all in a line,
As frogs leap and croak, claiming each vine.

The beavers clap paws, in perfect sync,
With wiggly worms dancing, who'd ever think?
The starlings swoop low, in choreographed flights,
Bringing laughter and joy to those woodland nights.

A coyote howls out, a mistaken lead,
The hedgehogs huddle close, plotting their seed.
Such joyous wild rhythms, each hilarious note,
In the choir of the woodlands, all creatures emote.

So sway with the breeze, let your spirit run free,
In this whimsical realm, join the woodland spree.
Where melodies echo through each floral nook,
In our merry commune, a joyous storybook.

Lullabies of the Silent Grove

In the quietest grove, where whispers play,
The slumbering critters shake off the day.
A bear softly snores, a laugh in his dream,
While the owls keep watch, plotting their scheme.

The shy little mice hum a soft, sweet tune,
As stars play peekaboo behind the full moon.
A sleepy old tortoise starts to sway,
In a drowsy ballet, he dreams the night away.

Even the branches rock in gentle embrace,
While shadows dance slowly, tiptoeing in space.
Each rustle and whisper a lullaby sweet,
Nature's own choir, where silence finds beat.

So if you wander near, come join the sleep fest,
Where giggles and dreams make for laughter's best.
In this soothing cocoon, the woodland's a-bloom,
With giggling lullabies in the stillness of gloom.

Soliloquy of the Sylvan

In the woods where whispers play,
Trees chat over lemonade,
Branches swinging, quite a sight,
Squirrels dancing, hearts alight.

Fungi giggle, mushrooms poke,
Old birch grumbles, cracks a joke,
Leaves applaud with rustling cheer,
Nature's laughter fills the sphere.

Grasshoppers sing in quirky tones,
Kissing bees share silly moans,
Twilight's glow, a teasing wink,
Sunset hues in shades of pink.

As night falls, a raccoon jives,
Bopping under starry skies,
The moon chuckles, all is right,
In this woods, such pure delight.

The Soundtrack of the Swaying Pines

Whistling winds play favorite tunes,
Pines sway gently, shake their moons,
A woodpecker joins the beat,
While rabbits hop to a funky feat.

A babbling brook's a clever rap,
With splashes making quite the clap,
The owls hoot a jazz-filled night,
Their rhythms keeping spirits bright.

Mice step lightly for a waltz,
As squirrels join without a fault,
Each branch bounces like it knows,
This forest's fun, it ebbs and flows.

When morning comes, the chorus ends,
But laughter lingers with good friends,
A symphony of life's embrace,
In the pines, we find our place.

Serenes of the Syringa

In bloom the lilacs take a bow,
While crickets dance, and take a vow,
To serenade the buzzing bees,
That flutter 'round with goofy ease.

With fragrant scents that fill the air,
The flowers giggle without care,
In gardens neat, the rabbits frolic,
While daisies chat in words symbolic.

A butterfly sporting polka dots,
Looks for friends in sunny spots,
The roses blush, they feel so sly,
As wind carries a playful sigh.

At dusk, the crickets start their show,
While fireflies join, putting on a glow,
Together they paint the night sky bright,
In lilac land, all feels just right.

The Cadence of Verdant Dreams

Amidst the green, the grasses sway,
With whispers of the breezy play,
Frogs croak out syncopated lines,
While trees connect like clever vines.

A badger dons a tiny hat,
And struts around, so fancy that,
The hedgehogs chuckle, join the jam,
As dandelions wave "Bam! Bam!"

In the clear, a rain cloud winks,
While cute little faeries share their drinks,
They giggle as they splash about,
Each drop a note, each laugh a shout.

With twilight's end, the concert fades,
And nature sleeps in leafy shades,
But dreams of fun will not depart,
For in the woods, there's always heart.

Shadows in the Canopy

Underneath the branches wide,
Squirrels dance and glide.
A raccoon with a silly grin,
Tries to wear a hat made of tin.

The shadows twist and play around,
As the winds create a sound.
A bird, with flair, falls out of tune,
Sings loudly with a silly croon.

The sun peeks through the leafy maze,
Bunnies hop in a dazed haze.
A deer prances, quite absurd,
Mimicking a dancing bird.

Giggling leaves get lost in cheer,
As friends join in with a cheer.
Nature's jesters, all around,
In the trade of laughter found.

Melodies from the Forest Floor

Mushrooms grow like little hats,
While ants march like tiny brats.
A frog croaks a jazzy beat,
While stomping on his webbed feet.

Beetles glide with fancy flair,
As critters join the funny air.
Snakes wiggle, feeling slick,
Living life just like a trick.

Furry friends all gather near,
Planning games with lots of cheer.
A picnic with leaves as plates,
In nature's realm, there are no fates.

Each corner holds a raucous joke,
From playful leaves and gentle smoke.
A world where laughter freely pours,
On the ground, oh what a score!

April's Choral Awakening

April showers bring a throng,
Of blooming blooms that hum along.
Woeful worms begin to sway,
As petals join the bright ballet.

Buds burst forth with vibrant glee,
While flowers giggle, 'Look at me!'
A butterfly flaps by with flair,
Landing on a teddy bear.

In the breeze, a jolly tune,
The blooms all hum beneath the moon.
Grass blades shimmy to the beat,
Inviting all to tap their feet.

Bumblebees with tiny hats,
Buzz along like chubby cats.
How nature loves a merry day,
In every laugh, a bright display.

Crescendos of Earth and Sky

Raindrops plunk like little drums,
As clouds above, they wiggle, hum.
A squirrel twirls through liquid air,
Jumps, then lands in a puddle there.

Thunder claps with a silly grin,
As lightning strikes; let the fun begin!
Everyone knows, at this time,
A dance-off starts, oh, how sublime!

A chorus of frogs takes the stage,
Each one wearing a little page.
With ribbits loud and leaps so grand,
They serenade this lovely land.

As colors mix in the sky's embrace,
Nature giggles in a wild race.
Here we find, in every sigh,
The joyous echoes of earth and sky.

The Call of the Cedar

In the forest, a loud cheer,
A tree that jokes, oh dear!
Branches wave, they share the tease,
Sprightly limbs in a gentle breeze.

Squirrels dance on bark so sly,
Telling tales that make you cry.
Sap drips down like sticky gum,
Laughing now, who was that dumb?

Roots take turns in a silly race,
Trying hard to find their place.
Pinecone prizes, yes, they fight,
Cedar grins, "This feels just right!"

Snap! A branch joins in the fun,
Nature's circus, everyone!
With every rustle, we can see,
The humor of the great green spree.

Dancing with the Wind

Leaves are twirling, what a show,
They whisper secrets, soft and low.
The breeze comes creeping, full of fright,
Yet the trees sway, all with delight.

Bark is grinning, what a sight,
Branches bobbing left and right.
A woodpecker joins with a tap,
Swinging to nature's funny clap.

The clouds are giggling overhead,
Making shadows dance, it's said.
Roots stick out, do the twist,
Who knew trees could do this?

The melody of rustling leaves,
Brings a chuckle, as it weaves.
Underneath a sky so grand,
We dance together, hand in hand.

Harmonies of Nature's Tapestry

In the patchwork of the woods,
Laughter echoes, all feels good.
With a twist and turn of the vine,
Every leaf is a friend of mine.

A chorus of critters takes their place,
Even the mushrooms join the race.
Singing songs that make us grin,
As the sun sets, let the fun begin!

Twigs snap like funny little beats,
Nature's rhythm, oh, what treats!
Bumblebees hum a silly tune,
While frogs croak as if they swoon.

Caterpillars wiggle and roll,
In this wood, they play their role.
With every step, laughter we find,
A symphony of joy combined.

Trills Beneath the Twigs

Beneath the twigs, the critters meet,
A party starting, what a feat!
With chirps and squeaks, they gather 'round,
The funniest friends are always found.

A turtle spins in perfect place,
While rabbits join the silly race.
Under bushes, they poke their heads,
Squealing laughter, who needs beds?

A lizard does a little dance,
Critters giggle, here's their chance.
With a shimmy and a shake so spry,
Nature's joke is not too shy.

Wiggly worms sing low and long,
Their squirmy tune is not so wrong.
In this wood of joyful jests,
The rhythms of fun are the best!

Harmonious Gestures of Growth

In a forest where trees take stance,
The spruces do a funny dance.
They twirl their branches, oh what a scene,
Like nature's jesters, living the dream.

With roots that tickle the earth below,
They giggle and wiggle, putting on a show.
Their needles whisper secrets and cheer,
Like comedians who laugh without fear.

Beneath the boughs of the tallest spruces,
The critters join in with their own excuses.
A squirrel juggles acorns with zest,
While a wise old owl just takes a rest.

Then come the winds, with a playful shove,
Inviting the trees to dance with love.
They sway and they shimmy, side to side,
In their green-topped hats, they take great pride.

The Symphony of Seasons

In springtime's bloom, the trees come alive,
Dressed in green gowns, they jive and thrive.
They chuckle at snowflakes still hanging near,
Making winter blush, it's time for cheer.

Summer's here, with sun's golden rays,
The spruces are sunbathing, what a craze!
They wear shades and sip on dew from leaves,
Telling tall tales of summer eves.

When autumn shows up with colors bold,
The trees flex their needles, looking gold.
They toss their pinecones, what a funny plight,
As squirrels prepare for a nutty night.

Winter approaches, a cold icy blast,
The spruces are wrapped in blankets so vast.
They chuckle with frost, in coats oh so white,
Counting the days till spring's first light.

Forest Fugues

In the heart of the woods, where shadows convene,
The spruces perform, shifting their green.
They host a grand concert, with birds as the choir,
As squirrels accompany, climbing higher and higher.

A raccoon on drums, he keeps the beat,
While a chipmunk sings, oh so sweet.
The melody sways with each rustling leaf,
Bringing out giggles, what crazy relief.

They share silly stories of seasons gone by,
The spruce trees chuckle, and let out a sigh.
With roots in the ground, their laughter ring,
A timbre of joy that makes the heart sing.

As night falls gently, the stars start to twinkle,
The forest keeps laughing, with each little crinkle.
Together they create a symphonic spree,
A concert of friendship, wild and free.

Breezes of the Ancient Pines

In ancient pines, where winds love to roam,
The trees tell tales of their childhood home.
With each breeze blowing, they sway to the tune,
Spinning stories beneath the bright moon.

Their needles laugh softly, with secrets in tow,
As rabbits pass by, doing a hop and a flow.
The pines tease the critters, with whispers of jest,
In their wise, woody voices, they are truly blessed.

As the sun dips low, they share silly facts,
About raindrops' dances and clouds' quirky acts.
The forest echoes with giggles of glee,
While the ancient pines sway, feeling quite free.

So when you wander, give a shout to the trees,
Join in their laughter, let's sway with the breeze.
For in every giggle, there's joy to be found,
In the heart of the forest, life spins round and round.

www.ingramcontent.com/pod-product-compliance
Lightning Source LLC
Chambersburg PA
CBHW071830160426
43209CB00003B/266